What to Say: 12 Major Gift Asks to Get a YES

Proven word-for-word scripts to land the gift

Mary Petersen

Contents

For Carol

You may not remember me, but I'll never forget you. You gave me my very first face-to-face "no." For the next few days, it crushed me — tears, doubts, questioning whether I was even cut out for this career. But your "no" became my rite of passage. It launched me on a multi-year quest to refine my ask, to learn how to turn a no into a maybe, and a maybe into a yes.

Carol, you were gracious, kind, and honest — even in saying no. And in doing so, you gave me a greater gift: the spark that shaped the fundraiser (and coach) I am today. Thank you.

Want to see the entire Carol story? Scan the QR Code below:

A Note from Mary

For many years, I only knew one way to ask for a gift. I used the same approach with every donor, regardless of their personality, style, or interests. It was my go-to.

Sometimes it worked. Sometimes it didn't. But it always felt harder than it needed to be.

About 15 years into making asks, I started to notice something: donors don't all give for the same reasons.

Some give from their **head**: they want stats, budgets, impact numbers, and clear evidence that their gift will be effective.

Others give from their **heart**: they want to feel something, hear stories, and connect emotionally with the people they'll be helping.

And some give from their **gut**: they get a good feeling about you, the staff, the program, or the organization, and they trust that instinct.

When I started matching the way I asked to the way the donor gave — head, heart, or gut — everything shifted. The yeses came quicker. The nos stung less. And asking became easier, even joyful.

Fundraiser, my socks were rolling up and down when I realized I didn't have to use the same ask with every donor; I could tailor my ask to meet them where they are.

That's one reason I wrote this book. Because fundraising isn't just about knowing *what* to ask for, it's about learning *how* to ask in a way that meets your donor where they are.

I hope that this book becomes your playbook, a companion you can return to again and again when preparing for a solicitation. Because when you learn to match the style of your ask to the style of your donor, you'll find yourself hearing "yes" more often, and with far more joy along the way.

Here's to your next joyful yes,
Mary

P.S. Don't miss the **What to Say Resource Hub!** It's your (free) online companion to put this book into action. Inside you'll get **ready-to-use swipe files, simple checklists, quick coaching audios,** and **invitations to live practice sessions** (with replays). It's everything you need to try the language, prep fast, and raise more money. Check it out at wts.heyfundraiser.com.

Part I:

. . . .

The Foundation

Chapter One:
Why Asking Is the Missing Link

Fundraiser, let's start with a confession: I love fundraising books.

There are hundreds of them on my shelves and in my Kindle library, and many of them are brilliant. Books about the psychology of giving, building donor relationships, stewardship that creates loyalty, and the history and philosophy of philanthropy. Some of these works have shaped me as a fundraiser and as a person.

And let me be clear: those books are necessary. They've paved the way for generations of fundraisers to approach donors with more wisdom, empathy, and strategy.

But here's the gap I kept seeing: very few of those books tell you exactly what to say when you're sitting across from a donor and it's time to ask for the gift.

That's the moment most fundraisers dread. That's the moment that makes your palms sweat and your heart race. And yet, there aren't many books about it, and it's the moment that changes everything.

The Missing Link

I've been a major gift fundraiser for over 25 years. I've seen magnificent cultivation strategies, moving stewardship reports, and gala dinners that could win awards. But here's the truth:

None of it matters if you don't actually **make the ask.**

Cultivation without solicitation is just a friendship. Stewardship without solicitation is just good customer service. At some point, Fundraiser, you've got to look your donor in the eye and say:

"Would you consider a gift of $250,000 to make this happen?" That's the missing link.

A Story to Start Us Off

I once worked with a family who adored our mission. They toured our programs, they met our staff, and they even volunteered. They were *all in*.

The day came to ask for their support. I'll be honest: I was nervous. I could have tiptoed around the ask. I could have hedged. Instead, I took a deep breath, looked them in the eye, and said:

"Joe and Leonora, would you consider a gift of $1 million to name the new health center pavilion?"

There was a pause. My heart pounded. Then they smiled. "Yes. We'd be honored. We can't think of a better way to give back to the community we love so much."

It wasn't magic. It was clarity. It was having the courage to put a number and a program on the table.

Why This Book Is Different

So here's what this book is not: it's not meant to replace the incredible work of thought leaders who have written about donor-centered fundraising, relationship-building, or transformational stewardship. If you haven't read those books, you should. They will give you wisdom and grounding. You won't find 300 pages on cultivation here. You won't find theories about strategies. What you'll find is something rarer: a practical, use-this-today verbiage toolkit.

Here's what those books rarely give you: the words. At the end of the day, the words matter. The difference between "support us at whatever level feels right" and "would you consider $100,000 to fund the new hotline?" is like comparing apples and orangutans.

One is vague. The other is clear. One gets a polite smile. The other gets a decision. One leaves the donor wondering what you really need. The other invites them to step directly into impact. One will result in a "maybe." One will get you a "yes."

This book is about giving you the words, the phrases, the scripts, the confidence to walk into a room and know exactly how you're going to ask.

My Promise

By the time you turn the last page, you will have:

- 12 distinct ask styles (with multiple variations for each).
- Real-life examples across nonprofits: hospitals, food banks, arts & culture, youth programs, faith communities, domestic violence shelters, cancer research, and more.
- Coaching tips to help you practice until the words feel natural.
- A consolidated toolkit for handling objections with confidence.

Fundraiser, you won't just know *why* to ask; you'll know exactly *what to say*. First, we'll tackle the biggest mistakes fundraisers make in the ask (so you can avoid them). Then we'll break down the anatomy of a strong ask. And finally, we'll get into the fun part: the scripts. By the end, you'll never walk into a donor meeting empty-handed again. High five!

Chapter Two:
The 5 Elements of a Strong Ask

Asking for a major gift can feel intimidating, but every effective solicitation follows the same rhythm. Once you understand that rhythm, you'll never feel like you're winging it again.

There are five elements: the set-up, the ask, the silence, the donor's response, and the fundraiser's response. Master these five, and you'll have a framework you can trust every single time. Let's go through them.

The Set-Up

The set-up is how you prepare the donor for the conversation. Too many fundraisers skip this step and end up surprising the donor, which breaks trust.

Sometimes the set-up happens at the very beginning of the solicitation meeting. However, it's even better when it happens during the call or meeting beforehand—that way, the donor walks into the meeting prepared and expecting the ask.

Examples:

- "Next time we meet, I'd love to talk with you about a significant commitment to the program you love."
- "When we come back together, I'd like to bring a proposal for your consideration. Would that be okay?"
- "Would you be open to us talking about a potential leadership gift at our next conversation?"

When you signal what's coming, you show respect and give your donor the chance to prepare, which dramatically increases the likelihood of a positive response.

When you skip the set-up, you increase the chances of hearing "no." If a donor isn't ready, it's far better for them to tell you that in advance than in the middle of a solicitation. By asking permission, "Next time we meet, I'd love to bring a proposal for your consideration. Would that be okay?" you allow the donor to signal if the timing isn't right. That way, you avoid putting both of you in an awkward spot. The set-up protects the relationship and keeps the solicitation moment transparent, respectful, and collaborative.

The Ask

This is the heart of the moment. And it always follows the same formula:

First Name + Invitation + Specific Amount + Program/Fund

That's it. That's the anatomy of the ask sentence. The *invitation* is crucial. Phrases like *"Would you consider…," "What would it take for you to consider…,"* or *"Under what circumstances might you…"* are respectful, curious, and open-ended. They invite the donor into a decision instead of boxing them in. That simple shift changes the energy of the moment. Instead of feeling pressured, the donor feels engaged.

Examples:

- "David, would you consider $50,000 to provide summer camp scholarships for 100 kids who would otherwise be home alone?"
- "Emily, would you consider a gift of $200,000 to establish a patient assistance fund so no one goes without life-saving medication this year?"
- "Michael, would you be open to a $1 million gift to endow a faculty chair in the environmental science department?"

The name anchors attention. The amount shows confidence. The program ties the gift back to your mission.

Want to Know How to Choose the Ask Amount?

Most fundraisers struggle with *how much* to ask for — and it's one of the biggest reasons good asks fall flat. Scan this QR code to access my companion course, **Precision Asking: How to Set the Perfect Ask Amount.** You'll learn the framework I use to calculate, test, and confidently present the right number every time.

The Silence

To you, it feels like an eternity. I've sat there with cold sweat dripping down my back, with every nerve in my body screaming: *Say something, fill the space, rescue the moment.*

But what feels like agony for you is simply processing time for the donor. They're weighing commitments, obligations, values, and priorities. That pause is not awkward for them; it's necessary.

Here's what silence really means: the donor is taking you seriously. They're considering what you've asked, running the numbers in their head, picturing the impact, and imagining what this commitment would mean for their life. That's not rejection. That's discernment.

You may even see the wheels turning: eyes glance up as they calculate, they shift in their seat, or they look down for a moment to think. These are good signs. It means your request has been received and they're giving it real attention.

The temptation in those ten seconds is to panic and talk yourself out of the gift: *"But if that number is too high, we could always go lower…"* Don't do it. Once you break the silence, you interrupt their decision-making process and weaken your own ask.

So hold the quiet. Breathe. Take a sip of water. Count slowly in your head. Ten seconds may feel like ten years, but those seconds are where the decision is happening.

What's Happening in the Donor's Mind During the Silence

While you're sweating through ten seconds of silence, here's what your donor may actually be thinking:

- *"How will this affect the pledge I'm paying off for another organization. Can I layer this on top?"*
- *"My twins have two years left of college, how does that affect my giving right now?"*
- *"This is more than I had planned… but could I make it work over a few years?"*
- *"What impact would this gift have compared to the other causes I support?"*
- *"Do I want to step into this level of leadership with this organization?"*
- *What investments are coming due this quarter?*
- *Did I take the Required Minimum Distribution from my IRA this year? Could I devote that to making this gift?*

In other words, they're not ignoring you, and they're not offended. They're giving your ask the serious consideration it deserves.

The Donor's Response

Eventually, the donor speaks. And this is where the real work begins.

In my 25+ years of major gift work, I've learned that donors respond in all kinds of ways: some expected, some surprising. The important thing to remember is this: a response is a sign of engagement. It means they've heard you, they're taking your ask seriously, and they're now doing the mental and emotional work of deciding how to step in.

Here are the most common responses you'll hear:

Immediate yes: "Yes, I'd be honored to do that."

Conditional yes: "I can do it if the timing works out the way I expect."

Stretch yes: "That's more than I planned, but I'll find a way."

Counteroffer: "I can't do $1 million, but I could do $500,000."

Installments: "I could do it over five years instead of all at once."

Need more info: "Can you show me exactly how the money will be used?"

Need time: "I'll need to talk it over with my spouse."

Deferral: "Let's revisit this in six months."

Different interests: "That program isn't where my heart is. Do you have other opportunities?"

Soft no: "It's not possible for me right now."

Hard no: "I'm not interested in supporting this."

Every one of these responses is valid. Some open the door wider, some close it for now, and some simply redirect you to another path. Your role is not to judge them or take the answer personally. Your role is to listen, respect what's being offered, and respond with grace and professionalism.

Remember: the donor's response, no matter how brief, means you've done your job. You brought the donor to a decision point. That is success. You can't control the outcome, but you can control how you show up in the moment. If you stay calm, clear, and grateful, even a "no" can move the relationship forward.

The Fundraiser's Response

Once the donor has spoken, your role shifts. This is where many fundraisers fumble: either by rushing, over-explaining, or showing disappointment. But this moment is just as important as the ask itself.

The donor's response is a gift, regardless of its form. They've engaged with you. They've revealed something about their priorities, their capacity, or their timing. Your job is to meet that response with composure, respect, and gratitude.

Below are the most common responses I've heard in over 25 years of major gift work, along with suggestions on how you, the fundraiser, can respond in a way that builds trust and keeps the relationship moving forward.

Response Type	Donor's Response	Fundraiser's Response
Immediate yes	"Yes, I'd be honored to do that."	Pause. Smile. Thank them warmly: "Thank you, this means so much. We're so excited to partner with you on…"
Conditional yes	"I can do it if the timing works out the way I expect."	Affirm: "That makes sense. Let's talk through what timing would feel right for you."
Stretch yes	"That's more than I planned, but I'll find a way."	Celebrate their generosity: "I'm humbled. Thank you for stepping up in such a big way."
Counteroffer	"I can't do $1 million, but I could do $500,000."	Thank them immediately: "That's incredibly generous. $500,0000 would be amazing. Here's the impact your gift will have…"
Installments	"I could do it over five years instead of all at once."	Embrace it: "Absolutely, spreading it out makes perfect sense. Let's set it up in a way that works best for you."

Need more information	"Can you show me exactly how the money will be used?"	Provide clarity: "Of course. Let me walk you through the budget so you can see exactly what your gift funds will support."
Need time	"I'll need to talk it over with my spouse."	Respect it: "Of course. Would it be helpful if I followed up in a few days after you've had that discussion?"
Deferral	"Let's revisit this in six months."	Agree and lock in: "That works. How about we schedule a check-in now for six months from today? And, in the meantime, I'll be sure to keep you updated periodically."
Different interest	"That program isn't where my heart is. Do you have others?"	Pivot with openness: "Of course! We want to match your philanthropy with the program you love the most. Can you tell me what areas really excite you? Let's explore where your passion fits."
Soft no	"It's not possible for me right now."	Honor it: "I understand. Thank you for considering it. Can we revisit this later, maybe in 6 months?"

| Hard no | "This just isn't something I believe in."

"We've decided our giving is going in a completely different direction."

"Your organization isn't on our priority list anymore."

"I'm not comfortable with the leadership/direction right now."

"We're cutting back our philanthropy significantly, and I won't be giving."

"I don't think this is the right fit for me." | Fundraiser, a "no" can sting, but it's still a gift of clarity. It means you can bless and release the energy of chasing this particular opportunity and redirect it to cultivating elsewhere. A 'no' today doesn't mean 'no' forever, but it does mean you have to respect the boundary the donor has clearly set.

Respond with grace: "Thank you for being candid. I respect your decision, and I'm grateful we had this conversation. I'd still love to keep you updated periodically, if that's okay. |

Your response is an opportunity to make a donor feel validated or dismissed. Remember, "not now" is not "not ever." When you respond with gratitude and composure, even a no becomes part of a longer, stronger relationship.

When the Response is Off-the-Wall (and Feels Personal)

Once in a blue moon, a donor's response will stop you in your tracks. I've heard things like:

- "I don't like your CEO's vision."
- "I think your board is weak."

- "Why would I give to you when XYZ organization does this better?"
- "Honestly, I don't believe in this project at all."
- "I'll give if you fire so-and-so."

These comments can feel like a punch to the gut because they're not just about the ask; they're about *your organization, your leadership, or your mission.*

Here's what you need to remember: stay calm, don't get defensive, and don't take it personally. The donor is giving you feedback, sometimes harshly, but it's feedback nonetheless.

A good response might sound like:

- "Thank you for being so candid. I'd love to understand more about what you mean."
- "I hear you. Leadership plays a crucial role in this. Let me take that back to the team."
- "I appreciate your honesty. Even if this project isn't a fit, I value your perspective."

The goal isn't to argue them into agreement. The goal is to stay composed, gather insight, and protect the relationship.

Putting It Together

Every strong ask has five elements: the set-up, the ask, the silence, the donor's response, and the fundraiser's response.

When you practice these, you'll stop dreading the ask and start trusting the process. Because in the end, asking is not about perfection. It's about clarity, respect, and courage.

Chapter Three:
How to Know When It's the Right Time to Ask

Fundraiser, this is the #1 question I hear from clients: "How do I know when to ask for a major gift?"

Not knowing the timing creates what I call *fundraiser purgatory*: endless coffees, serial cultivation, and overthinking every smile, nod, and email reply. Ask too soon, and you risk catching the donor off guard. Wait too long, and you may miss the sweet spot altogether.

The truth? There's no magic formula, no tea leaves, no cosmic signal. However, five clear signs indicate the donor is ready for the ask. You don't just need one or two of them. **You need all five working together.**

Each of these five readiness signs is equally important. They work like the legs of a table; take one away, and the whole thing wobbles. Take two away, and you don't trust it to hold a drink. If your table only has one or two legs, let's just sit on the floor. But when all five are in place, you can comfortably pull up a seat at the table, stop second-guessing yourself, and move forward with confidence.

1. You Have Permission to Ask for a Major Gift

I wholeheartedly believe in permission-based fundraising. When I started using the concept, my fundraising skyrocketed. Permission-based fundraising is agreeing to the next steps with a donor at every interaction. That way, you and the donor are always on the same page. At the end of each call, email, text, or meeting, I would say, "Ellen, can I follow up with you in two weeks when you're back from vacation?" "Sophia, could I bring our program director with me next time we meet? I think you'd enjoy hearing from her directly. I'll get it on the books for next month, if that works for you." "Marcus, can I check in with you after the gala to get your thoughts on what resonated most?"

Just make sure you do what you say you're going to do. Nothing breaks down trust quicker than not following through.

Before every solicitation meeting, I'll ask the donor *at the prior meeting or on the prior call*, "Would you be open to talking about a significant gift at our next meeting?" In most cases, the donor said yes. It's not about perfect timing. It's not about cultivating for years and years until the stars align. It's about clarity and trust. Permission is the signal that the donor is prepared for the conversation, and once you have it, you don't need to keep waiting.

A simple setup, such as "At our next conversation, I'd love to talk about a potential leadership gift. Would that be okay?" gives your donor the dignity of knowing what's ahead.

For my younger fundraising friends reading this book, please don't ask permission over a text. You need to hear the person's voice when they say "yes" or "no," so that you can decipher the tone and have a verbal exchange about their answer.

Sometimes Permission Speeds Things Up

Here's the funny thing about permission-based fundraising: sometimes when you ask for permission, the donor doesn't want to wait. Why? Because giving is awesome!

You might say, *At our next conversation, I'd love to talk with you about a significant gift. Would that be okay?* And the donor responds, *Why wait? What do you have in mind?* (I swoon when donors say this!)

That's why you never show up empty-handed. Even if you expected a simple set-up meeting, have your ask amount and script ready to go. Because when a donor leans in like that, you want to meet the moment, not fumble it.

2. You Know Their Capacity to Give & How Much to Ask For

You don't need to know the exact size of someone's bank account, but you should have a realistic sense of whether the level you're about to ask for is within reach. Capacity clues can come from giving history to your organization, career success, business ownership, lifestyle, or their generosity with other organizations. One tell-tale sign is that they are giving large gifts to other organizations.

On the flip, don't assume someone "can't give" just because they don't flash wealth. The "millionaire next door" is a real thing! Likewise, don't undersolicit a donor you know has the means. Asking for far less than they can comfortably give isn't polite; it's dismissive. It tells them you haven't done your homework, or worse, that you don't see their potential.

Fundraiser, many of our peers are worried about asking for too much and running the risk of upsetting the donor. Most donors won't be offended if you ask higher than they can manage. Many are actually flattered and will say, "Wow. I'm honored that you think I can give that much!" They'll counter, or they'll stretch. That's why capacity is a readiness sign; when you know they *could* do it, you can ask boldly and let them calibrate from there.

3. You Understand What Motivates Their Giving

Every donor has a "why." Some want to honor their parents. Some want to make their community better. Some give because it is a deeply spiritual act. Some want to inspire others to take a step forward. Some want to leave a legacy. And some, yes, are motivated by tax strategy or naming opportunities.

Knowing a donor's motivation is like holding the key to the door. You discover it by asking good questions during cultivation:

- "What inspired your past philanthropy?"
- "What change do you want to make in the world?"
- "How do you hope people will remember your generosity?"

When you understand *why* they give, you can shape the ask so it resonates. A donor who wants to leave a legacy might consider an endowed scholarship or a naming opportunity. A donor who wants leverage will perk up at a challenge match. A donor who cares about immediate needs will get excited about emergency relief.

Motivation is a readiness sign because it shows you're not guessing. You're aligning the ask with their personal "why."

4. You Know Why They Give to Your Organization

Even the most passionate, wealthy, motivated donor won't say yes if they don't feel a *personal connection* to your work. The real question is: has your mission touched their life, their family, or someone they love?

That's the spark you're looking for. Maybe their mom battled cancer, and that's why they care about free mammograms. Maybe their daughter struggled in school, and that's why they light up when you talk about tutoring. Maybe they grew up hungry, and that's why they can't stand the thought of a child going without meals.

During your cultivation efforts, you can ask questions that will get you to the heart of their motivation: *What inspired your very first gift?* or *What part of our work feels closest to your heart?* The answers will tell you where their story intersects with your organization.

5. You Know Their Favorite Program/Project at the Organization

Capacity without passion is just wealth. Passion without capacity is enthusiasm. But when the two meet? Major gift magic.

You know you've hit passion when the donor's eyes light up talking about a program, when their voice rises as they share a personal connection, or when they ask, "How can I help?" These donors don't just admire your mission; they *feel a genuine connection to it.*

Passion is revealed in small moments: a donor tearing up during a site tour, asking detailed questions about one program (while ignoring the others), or following up with staff they've met. These are clues that this particular part of your work resonates deeply.

Your job is to match your fundraising ask to their passion. If they care about scholarships, don't pitch them a building. If they care about animals, don't ask them to fund parking lots. Passion points the way, and when you align your ask with what already matters to them, you're no longer persuading. You're partnering.

Bringing It Together

When you have all these answers, you're ready to rock and roll. It doesn't mean you'll always get a yes. But it does mean you're asking at the right time, in the right way, with integrity.

Fundraiser, just one more chapter before we get to the FUN stuff - the Scripts! Keep reading…

Chapter Four:
The Top Mistakes Fundraisers Make in the Ask

Asking for a major gift can be intimidating. The fear is real. I used to get stomach pain, severe anxiety, the shakes, and flop sweats (sometimes all at the same time!) until I grew out of it.

This is why you're scared: When you ask, you're putting yourself in a vulnerable space where you could get a "no." That possibility makes your heart race, your face flush, and your mouth go dry.

That fear is why so many fundraisers avoid the moment of truth. Instead, they hide in endless cultivation. They plan one more tour, one more coffee, one more update. They convince themselves they're "building the relationship" when really, they're stalling. I call this serial cultivation, and it's one of the most common ways we sabotage ourselves.

Here's the hard truth: cultivating forever doesn't guarantee a gift. Hoping the donor eventually offers one unprompted isn't fundraising. It's wishful thinking.

The only way forward is to ask. And when fear pushes us to dodge that responsibility, we slip into bad habits that weaken our asks when we finally make them.

The good news? These mistakes are predictable, and once you see them, you can avoid them.

Mistake #1: Apologizing or Hedging

Nothing weakens an ask faster than starting with, "I hate to ask, but…" or "Maybe you'd be comfortable with…" When you apologize, you signal that asking is something to be embarrassed about, when in fact, asking is a joyful invitation.

Weak ask: "I know you give to a lot of places, and this might not be the right time, but maybe you'd consider $10,000?"

Stronger alternative: "Tom, we're so honored to have you as a partner. Your philanthropy has a profound impact on many in our city.

As you think about your involvement this year, would you consider a gift of $10,000 to help us launch our new after-school STEM program for middle schoolers?"

One feels hesitant. The other is confident and clear.

Mistake #2: Being Vague

Vague asks are the kiss of death. "Support us at whatever level feels comfortable" is not an ask. It's a suggestion. And suggestions rarely move donors to action.

On the flip, this isn't the Cheesecake Factory menu either. Donors don't want 27 options. They want one confident invitation.

When you're vague or present too many options, you put the mental work back on the donor: What level is appropriate? What do they actually need? What would make a difference? Donors don't want homework. They want clarity. If you don't provide it, many will default to doing nothing.

Your job is to make the next step obvious. A clear number and a clear purpose show confidence and respect for the donor's time.

Weak version: "We'd love for you to join us in supporting our work however you see fit."

Clear version: "Lisa, would you consider $100,000 to fund an entire weekend of free spay and neuter clinics?"

Notice the difference? The vague version leaves the donor guessing. The clear version puts a bold, specific opportunity right on the table.

Mistake #3: Asking For Too Little

Out of fear of scaring away a donor, fundraisers often under-solicit. They think, *If I keep the number small, they'll be more likely to say yes.* But here's the truth: donors don't get offended when you ask for more than they can give. In fact, many are flattered.

Imagine this: you sit down with Mackenzie Scott and ask her for $5,000. That's weird, almost insulting. The amount has to match the donor's capacity and vision. Asking too low tells a donor you don't understand who they are or what they can do.

When you ask boldly, something powerful happens. Many donors respond with, "Wow. I can't believe you think I can give a million dollars (insert chuckle here). I can't do $1 million, but I could do $500,000." They don't storm out. They don't cut ties. They counter. And often, they stretch. However, don't always oversolicit. The key here is to ask for the right amount.

Undersoliciting: "David, could you give $10,000?" (when you have a relationship and know he's capable of $100,000+).

Bold Ask: "David, I know that breast cancer has affected your family in many ways. Would you consider $100,000 to fund a year of mammograms for women without insurance?"

Donors rise to meet vision, not timidity. If you play small, you invite a small response. If you lead with courage, you permit them to step into generosity they may never have considered on their own.

Mistake #4: Talking Too Much

After you ask, silence feels unbearable. So what do fundraisers do? They keep talking. They justify, explain, or even start lowering the number before the donor has had a chance to speak.

I'll never forget the first time I really held the silence. It was maybe five or ten seconds, but to me, it felt like five years. I could feel the cold sweat break out across my shoulders and begin to slide down my back as I sat there waiting slowly. Every instinct in me wanted to jump in, to fill the void with more information, more justification, anything.

Here's the thing: while you're panicking, your donor isn't. They're not sitting there judging you. They're processing. Their wheels are turning.

They may be thinking, I just made a big investment that's going to tie up my money for six months. Or, my granddaughter still has another year of college, and tuition is a stretch for me. Or, this is a lot, but I do love this cause. How can I make this work?

That pause, which feels like agony to you, is actually space for them to consider the weight of your request. It's not awkward from their perspective. It's thoughtful. It's respectful.

So when you ask, say the words — and then stop. Take a sip of water. Breathe. Count to ten in your head if you have to. Give them the dignity of time to think.

Because those five to ten seconds of silence are not empty; they're full. They're where the decision happens.

Mistake #5: Surprising the Donor

Nothing derails an ask faster than a donor who wasn't expecting it. If they think it's just a "friendly coffee" and you spring a six-figure solicitation on them, you'll break trust in an instant.

I've seen this happen, and it's painful. A fundraiser sits down, chats about the weather, gives a program update, and then — out of nowhere — blurts out, "Would you consider a $250,000 gift to support our new building?"

The donor freezes. Not because they don't care, but because they didn't see it coming. The result? The donor feels ambushed, and the relationship often takes a step backwards.

Here's the thing: donors are generous, but they don't like surprises. They want to feel prepared. They want to walk into a meeting knowing why they're there and what kind of conversation they're agreeing to have.

That's why permission-based fundraising is so important. It prevents ambushes by making the donor a partner in the process. Something as simple as:

"We have really exciting things happening with our food programs. I know that's the program you love the most. Next time we meet, I'd love to talk to you about a significant commitment to our food programs. Would that be okay?"

or

"I'd love to share a giving opportunity that might be a fit. Would you be open to that?"

It gives the donor a heads-up and the dignity of choice. I feel so passionate about this that I'm going to give you three absurd examples, but please know that springing an ask is just as absurd.

If you invite someone to your house for a casual dinner and then surprise them with 50 people waiting for a formal fundraiser, they'll feel blindsided. If you tell them in advance, they come prepared, and they will enjoy themselves more.

Imagine showing up for what you thought was a routine doctor's appointment, only to have the doctor say, "We're scheduling surgery today." You'd panic, not because you didn't trust the doctor, but because you weren't prepared.

It's like being handed a surprise final exam without ever being told one was coming. Even if you are familiar with the material, the lack of preparation leaves you feeling resentful and unprepared.

Fundraising works the same way. Surprises build walls. Transparency builds trust.

So never "sneak in" an ask. Prepare your donor. Signal what's coming. Invite, don't ambush.

Mistake #6: Forgetting to Use the Donor's Name

This one might sound small and almost trivial, but I promise you, it isn't. It took me years to learn this, and when I finally did, it changed the way my asks landed.

Using a donor's first name at the very beginning of your ask anchors the moment. It's like flipping on a spotlight. Their head comes up. They make eye contact. They lean in—the room shifts.

Here's what happens when you don't: you slip into autopilot. You say, *We're looking for partners who might consider...* and the donor's attention drifts. They glance at their watch. They think about their to-do list. You're talking *at them,* not *to them.*

But when you say, *Sarah, would you consider a gift of $100,000 to help fund the new MRI machine?* you pull them into the moment. Their name is a bridge. It makes the ask personal, direct, and unmistakably theirs to consider.

I've seen this over and over. Early in my career, I'd stumble into asks without using the donor's name, and I'd get polite nods, vague responses, and a lot of "let me think about it." Later, when I made their name the first word out of my mouth, the reaction shifted. People leaned forward. They asked follow-up questions. The yeses came faster.

Donors want to feel seen, not like one of a hundred people on a list. Starting with their name tells them: *This isn't just an ask. This is your moment, your invitation, your opportunity to make an impact.* So don't skip it. Write it into your ask formula. Practice it. Make it second nature.

Weak version: "We're looking for partners who might consider a leadership gift of $100,000 to fund this program."

Stronger version: "David, your leadership has been vital to this church for decades. Would you consider a leadership gift of $100,000 to build the new fellowship hall?"

One is generic. The other is unmistakably personal.

Mistake #7: Losing Confidence at the Finish Line

This is the silent saboteur. You've done everything right: cultivated the relationship, understood the donor's motivations, identified the right project, and prepared the ask. You're right there, ready to step into the moment, and then your confidence falters.

It can happen in subtle ways. Your voice dips. You lower the number. You tack on, "But of course, whatever works for you." You hedge. And just like that, the clarity and strength of your ask evaporates.

Donors can feel it. They sense when you shrink back, and it makes them hesitate, too. If you're not confident in your own ask, why should they be confident in saying yes?

But here's the flip side: when you walk into that room with conviction, something powerful happens. You remind the donor that this isn't just about money. It's about possibility. It's about unleashing generosity that changes lives, saves families, and strengthens communities.

Fundraiser, do you realize what you get to do? You facilitate the conversations that change the world. You are the bridge between a donor's resources and the impact that reshapes lives forever. Hospitals get built. Food banks expand. Students go to college. Violence survivors find safety. Churches grow and thrive. Research accelerates.

None of that happens without someone, you, sitting across from a donor and saying with confidence: "Would you consider a gift of $250,000 to make this possible?"

That's not begging. That's leadership. That's courage. That's you leaning into the incredible privilege of this profession.

When your knees shake and your voice wavers, remember this: the work you're asking the donor to fund is too important for timidity. You owe it to your mission, to your community, and to your donor to stand tall and deliver the ask with confidence.

Because when you do, you're not just making an ask. You're opening the door to transformation. Don't we have the best job in the world?!

Bonus: Coaching Tips to Build Confidence

Confidence is a muscle, and like any muscle, it strengthens with practice. Here are simple ways to rehearse your asks until they feel natural:
- **Record yourself on your phone:** No one will see it, and you can delete it after, but hearing yourself back is the fastest way to catch hesitation, filler words, or weak phrasing.
- **Practice with a spouse or partner:** They don't need to know the ins and outs of fundraising; their feedback on your tone and confidence is enough.
- **Call your mom (or a trusted friend).** Say the words out loud to someone who's rooting for you. It will feel less scary when you sit down with a donor.

- **Stand in front of a mirror:** Watch your facial expressions and posture as you deliver the ask. Are you shrinking back or sitting tall?
- **Rehearse with a colleague:** Role-play the donor and fundraiser so you can both sharpen your asks.
- **Write the ask word-for-word:** Put pen to paper, then say it aloud ten times until it rolls off your tongue.
- **Use silence in practice:** Ask, then count to ten before speaking again. Get comfortable with the space that feels awkward but is actually powerful.
- **Find your "pump-up" ritual:** I used to have a song I'd play in the car on the way to every ask. It was my song. It got me in the right headspace, reminded me I could do this, and helped me walk into the meeting with confidence. I even had a little dance. Find what centers you and make it part of your routine. (Yes, all my colleagues made fun of me because of the song choice.)

The point isn't to memorize a script. It's to train your body and voice so the ask feels natural, calm, and confident when it matters most.

Need a "Pump-You-Up Playlist" to get you in the headspace for a big ask? Scan the QR code below.

Part II:
· · · · · · · · · ·
The Scripts

Chapter Five:
Matching the Ask to the Donor

Fundraiser, you now know why asking matters (Part I) and how to structure the moment (the five elements). However, none of it works unless you understand the person across from you.

Donors don't all give for the same reasons. After more than 25 years in major gifts, I've come to see that most giving decisions fall into three categories. When you match your ask to the donor's style, everything shifts. The yeses come quicker. The conversations flow more easily. And even the nos sting less, because you know you were speaking their language.

Category 1: Donors Who Give from Their Heads

These donors want clarity, precision, and evidence. They are analytical, data-driven, and often highly successful in business or technical fields. They want to know the organization is efficient, effective, and that the results are measurable.

They ask things like:

- "What percentage of my gift goes directly to the program?"
- "How do you measure success?"
- "Can I see your financials?"

They respond best to:

- Direct, specific asks
- Clear outcomes and metrics
- Confidence in your numbers

Category 2: Donors Who Give from Their Hearts

These donors are empathetic. They connect through narrative, emotion, and relationships. They want to *feel* a sense of fulfillment when they give. They are deeply motivated by creating change for the clients you serve.

They ask things like:

- "Tell me about the families you serve."
- "How does this program change lives?"
- "What difference does it make for real people?"

They respond best to:

- Stories with names and faces
- Gratitude for what they've already made possible
- Opportunities to connect their gift to human transformation

Category 3: Donors Who Give from Their Gut

These donors rely on intuition. They give when something feels right: the chemistry with you, the leadership of the organization, or the sense that this project is needed now. They don't always need all the details, but they need confidence in *you.*

They ask things like:

- "Who else is supporting this?"
- "Why now?"
- "Do I believe in this leader?"

They respond best to:

- Big vision and bold confidence
- Invitations to be part of shaping the future
- Exclusive opportunities or catalytic roles

Blended Donors: Most People Are a Mix

Few donors live 100% in one category. Many blend head, heart, and gut, an engineer who tears up at stories, a visionary who still wants the numbers, or a gut-truster who occasionally wants validation from the data. *That's why listening is everything.* If you notice them leaning into metrics, or adjusting their head. If they lean forward when you tell a story, stay with the heart. If they say, "This just feels right," don't drown them in spreadsheets.

Bringing It Together

The most powerful ask is the one that meets the donor where they are. Before you choose a script, ask yourself:

- Am I speaking to this donor's head?
- Am I speaking to this donor's heart?
- Am I speaking to this donor's gut?

When you match the style of your ask to the style of your donor, the conversation feels less like persuasion and more like alignment. That's when the yes comes easily, not because you mastered a script, but because you truly understood the person across the table.

Chapter Six:
The Direct Ask
(For Straight Shooters)

Some donors don't want the build-up. They don't want a 20-minute preamble, a binder full of charts, or a sweeping story. They want you to look them in the eye and ask.

The **Direct Ask** is just that — direct. It's short, specific, and clear. For the right donor, it's a relief. It communicates respect for their time and shows confidence in both the project and in them.

This style isn't for everyone, but it's ideal for individuals who are decisive, analytical, and prefer efficiency over lengthy explanations. Think engineers or entrepreneurs. Think accountants. Think of people who email you one-line responses.

When to Use It

- When the donor values speed and says things like, "Bottom-line it for me."
- When the project is tangible and straightforward.
- When the donor has already been cultivated and is ready for the conversation.

Verbiage Examples

"Robert, would you consider a gift of $100,000 to help us purchase a new MRI machine for our hospital?"

"Michael, would you consider $250,000 to launch a 24/7 hotline for survivors of domestic violence?"

"Lisa, would you consider $75,000 to expand our after-school hours so 85 kids have a safe place to go in the evenings this school year?"

Story of Success

Early in my career, I met with a retired engineer. He wasn't one for long conversations or emotional appeals; he valued precision and efficiency. I knew this because every coffee meeting we had was no more than 30 minutes long, and every email he sent me was one or two sentences long. When it came time to ask, I knew he would appreciate a direct approach:

"Robert, we need $100,000 to purchase a new MRI machine. The MRI was a $2M budgeted capital expense, but due to inflation, the cost increased, and we are now short. Would you be willing to fund the $100,000 gap?"

He paused, smiled, and said, "That's exactly the kind of clarity I like. Yes."

It was one of the easiest yeses of my career. Not because I had the perfect story, but because I matched my ask to his style.

Pitfalls to Avoid

- **Using too many words.** A direct-style donor doesn't want the TED Talk. They want clarity. If you circle the point, they'll tune out.
- **Overexplaining.** These donors don't need the long build-up. Spending even 10 minutes walking through the need before naming the number will leave them drained and impatient.
- **Softening the number.** "Maybe $100,000… or $50,000… or whatever works for you…" This signals insecurity and clashes with the donor's straightforward style.
- **Stacking options.** Offering multiple amounts or projects in one breath muddies the ask. Direct donors crave precision, not a buffet of options.

Fundraiser, the **Direct Ask** is clean. It's clear. And yes, it's gutsy. But for the right donor, it's exactly what they are waiting for.

Chapter Seven:
The Impact Ask
(For Donors Who Want to See Results)

Broad vision statements or emotional appeals don't move all donors. What they really want to know is: What will my gift do? These are the impact-driven donors. They want tangible outcomes, measurable results, and a clear sense that their dollars will make a difference.

The **Impact Ask** ties the donor's gift directly to the result. It translates generosity into lives touched, meals served, patients treated, or programs expanded. For these donors, it's not enough to say, "This will change lives." You have to show them how many and in what way.

They are invested in your work and probably know as much about your programs as you do. Picture the donors who read your annual reports for fun.

When to Use It

- When you have strong program data and can connect dollars to outcomes.
- When donors want specifics, not generalities.
- When a project's results are measurable in numbers, reach, or scale.

Verbiage Examples

"Ethan, a gift of $50,000 would stock the food pantry with 150,000 meals. That's enough to feed every family who walks through our doors from now through the holidays. Can we count on you?"

"Priya, will you consider an investment of $100,000, so we can operate a mobile dental clinic for an entire year? That's 1,200 children receiving preventative care who would otherwise go without."

"Marcus, a gift of $75,000 would expand our domestic violence shelter with 10 additional beds. That's 10 women and their children who will sleep safely each night instead of in their cars or on the streets."

Story of Success

I once met with a donor who asked me point-blank: "How do I know my gift will actually do something?"

Instead of brushing it off, I leaned in and said, "That's a fair question. Let me show you exactly what it looks like. A gift of $50,000 funds our literacy program for 200 kids this year. That ensures 200 children will read at or above their grade level, instead of falling behind. 200 families who won't have to wonder if their kids are ready for middle school. 200 futures that look brighter because you chose to step in."

The donor sat back in his chair. He thought for a moment, then said, "That's the first time I've felt like I could actually picture what my money does." And then he said yes.

That's the **Impact Ask** at work: clarity that gives the donor confidence their dollars aren't just disappearing into a void.

Pitfalls to Avoid

- **Drowning them in data.** Impact donors want numbers, but not a dissertation. If you present them with ten different statistics, it can become overwhelming. Keep it crisp.
- **Being vague.** "This will make a difference" won't cut it. Impact donors need a specific outcome to believe in.
- **Overpromising.** If you say their gift will "end hunger" or "eliminate homelessness," you'll lose credibility. Stay specific and truthful.
- **Making it transactional.** Impact is not about price tags. It's about transformation. Don't reduce their generosity to "buying units;" remind them their gift changes lives.

The **Impact Ask** reassures donors that their money matters in a tangible way. When you give them results to believe in, you give them the confidence to say yes.

Chapter Eight:
The Gratitude Ask
(For Longtime Supporters)

Some donors have already been on the journey with you for years. They've shown up, given faithfully, attended events, and maybe even volunteered. These donors want to know that their generosity hasn't just been noticed; it's mattered.

The **Gratitude Ask** honors the past while inviting the donor into the future. It begins with a genuine acknowledgment of what they've already done, then connects that impact to an opportunity to go even further.

These are your most loyal donors. Think "salt of the earth" supporters who have been with you through thick and thin. Remember donors who love to hear, "Because of you, this happened."

When to Use It

- With donors who have a long history of giving.
- When you can clearly name the impact of their past support.
- At milestone moments: anniversaries, new campaigns, expansions, or transitions.

Verbiage Examples

"Jamal, your generosity over the past decade has fueled this organization's growth. Because of you, thousands of families have had food on their tables. Would you consider $100,000 to help us open our new distribution center so we can reach even more?"

"Carlos, you've been with us since the very beginning. Thanks to your support, hundreds of students have attended college who otherwise wouldn't have had the opportunity. You have changed the trajectory of so many lives. A gift of $250,000 would enable us to establish scholarships for an additional 50 students. Is this something you would be interested in?"

"Margaret, your leadership gift five years ago made our clinic expansion possible. Because of you, families no longer have to drive 30+ minutes for their cancer treatment. They are closer to home. We're now focusing on improving the lives of children in our area. Would you join us again with $500,000 to launch our new pediatric unit?"

Story of Success

I once met with a longtime donor who had given faithfully for over 20 years. Instead of jumping straight into the need, I started by honoring him. "Because of you, 400 families had access to healthcare last year. Your generosity has literally changed the way this community thrives. Our community members are healthier and living better lives."

Then I invited him forward: "George, would you consider $100,000 to make sure even more families have that same access this year?" His eyes welled up. He didn't hesitate. He said yes.

That's the power of the **Gratitude Ask.** It transforms giving from obligation into celebration. Donors want to know that what they've already done mattered — and when they see that it did, they're eager to do more.

Pitfalls to Avoid

- **Making it about guilt.** "You've given so much, you could and should do more." Gratitude is an invitation, not a burden.
- **Being vague.** "Thanks for everything you've done, would you give again?" Without a specific story or outcome, the gratitude falls flat.
- **Overdoing the praise.** Gratitude should be sincere, not fawning.

If you pile it on too thick, it sounds manipulative.

- **Forgetting the "because of you."** This ask style only works when the donor sees how their past support led directly to impact.

The **Gratitude Ask** is about looking a donor in the eye and saying, "What you've done mattered. Here's how you can matter even more."

Chapter Nine:
The Partnership Ask
(For Donors Who Want to Be Part of the Team)

Some donors don't just want to give. They want to *join.* They want a seat at the table, to feel like their perspective matters, and to know they're shaping the future with you.

The **Partnership Ask** is about extending that invitation. It's not "we need your money," it's "we need you." This style of ask makes the donor feel like a co-creator, an insider, and a trusted partner in building what comes next.

Picture your entrepreneurs who enjoy taking an active role in building. Creative thinkers also appreciate this style. Imagine your community leaders who naturally lean into collaboration. Think of people who light up when they hear the words, "We see you as a partner in this."

When to Use It

- When the donor values influence and inclusion.
- When your organization is scaling or taking on a big new initiative.
- When you want to build long-term trust and a legacy.

Verbiage Examples

"Janet, your leadership has shaped this community in so many ways. We'd be honored to have you as a partner in the program development and launching our new youth innovation lab with a gift of $250,000."

"Arun, your insight has already guided so much of our work, specifically in helping us envision what multi-generational housing looks like. Would you consider taking your partnership one step further with a commitment of $500,000?"

"Nicole, your generosity has always gone beyond dollars. You've given your time, your wisdom, your energy. We count on your insight in so many ways. We'd love for you to partner with us by investing $100,000 to expand our community arts program, which will create more opportunities for emerging artists to learn, perform, and share their work."

Story of Success

A few years ago, I sat down with a longtime supporter to discuss a new youth program we were developing. Instead of just pitching it as a fully baked idea, I framed it as a partnership: "We'd love for you to be part of shaping this with us, and we see you as a partner in bringing it to life."

She leaned in. Not only did she commit the $500,000 we asked for, but she also actively participated in our planning sessions. She had connections to local schools we didn't have, ideas for curriculum we hadn't considered, and a perspective that made the program stronger.

The result? A youth initiative that was better designed, better connected to the community, and far more sustainable than what we had originally envisioned. And because she felt true ownership in the process, her commitment to the organization only deepened.

That's the power of the Partnership Ask. It doesn't just unlock resources; it invites donors to co-own impact.

Pitfalls to Avoid

- **Overpromising influence.** Don't imply that the donor will make decisions unless that's truly on the table. Empty promises will break trust.
- **Using "partner" too casually.** If everyone is a partner, the word

loses meaning. Reserve it for moments and donors where it really applies.

- **Confusing partnership with perks.** This isn't about gala tickets or VIP receptions. It's about vision, strategy, and impact.
- **Failing to back it up.** If you frame them as a partner, you need to actually treat them like one, through access, updates, and authentic inclusion.

The **Partnership Ask** is about belonging. It's about looking a donor in the eye and saying, "We can't do this without you, and we don't want to."

Chapter Ten:
The Missing Piece Ask
(For Donors Who Love to Finish the Puzzle)

Some donors thrive on being the one who gets you across the finish line. They love knowing that their gift is the final piece of the puzzle — the one that makes the vision whole.

The **Missing Piece Ask** frames the donor's gift as the essential last step. It's not about starting something from scratch; it's about completing something that's already in motion. For the right person, that's irresistible.

Envision problem-solvers, or the kind of donors who like to be the last in. Think people who get a thrill out of completing the picture and knowing that, *without them*, the job wouldn't be done.

When to Use It

- When you are near the end of a campaign or project and can show a clear funding gap.
- With donors who like urgency, clarity, and the satisfaction of completion.
- When you can quantify exactly what remains and why their gift will "seal the deal."

Verbiage Examples

"Darius, we are just $75,000 away from fully funding the renovation. Your gift could be the piece that gets us across the finish line."

"Leah, we've secured every part of the budget except for $250,000 to furnish and equip the space. Would you help us finish this project once and for all?"

"Victor, we've raised nearly all the funds needed to launch the new program. Your $50,000 gift would make it possible to start serving families immediately."

Story of Success

I once had a donor who always said, "Call me when you're close." So when we were down to the last $250,000 of a $4M campaign, I picked up the phone.

"Naomi, we're almost there. We have $250,000 left to meet our goal. Would you be the one to close the gap?"

She laughed and said, "That's my favorite role." She made the gift, and she was proud to know she was the one who brought the campaign across the finish line.

That's the **Missing Piece Ask**: it makes the donor the hero of the final chapter.

Pitfalls to Avoid

- **Stretching the truth.** If you're millions away and call it "almost there," donors will feel misled. The Missing Piece Ask only works when the gap is genuinely small (six-figures) and specific.
- **Being vague about the numbers.** "We just need a little more" doesn't cut it. These donors want precision: exactly how much, exactly what for.
- **Treating it like a discount.** This isn't about "what's left over;" it's about what's possible because the donor completes the picture. Don't make it sound like they're covering scraps.
- **Failing to celebrate their role.** Donors who close the gap want to be remembered as the finishers. If you don't acknowledge that, you miss the heart of this ask.

The **Missing Piece Ask** works because it lets the donor do something uniquely satisfying: finish what others have started and make the vision whole.

Chapter Eleven:
The Recognition Ask
(For Donors Who Value Legacy)

Some donors are deeply motivated by the chance to leave a mark. They want their name, or a loved one's, tied to something lasting. The **Recognition Ask** taps into that desire by offering donors a tangible, visible way to be remembered and honored.

This isn't about ego. For many, it's about family, legacy, or gratitude. It's about leaving something behind that tells the world, "We were here, and we cared."

Who are the families who've been pillars in the community? Consider your donors who speak about legacy and future generations. Think of people who want their children and grandchildren to walk past something with their name on it and feel proud.

When to Use It

- When naming opportunities exist, such as buildings, rooms, programs, endowments, or scholarships.
- With donors who talk about family, heritage, or "something to pass on."
- During major campaigns or capital projects in which recognition is a natural part of the giving structure.

Verbiage Examples

"Claudia, your leadership has already changed so many lives here. With a gift of $1 million, we would be honored to name the new community health pavilion in your family's honor."

"Samir, your generosity has made such a difference. Would you consider $250,000 to endow a scholarship in your parents' names so their legacy lives on?"

"Barbara, your family has been part of this congregation for three generations. A gift of $500,000 would allow us to dedicate the new fellowship hall as the *Smith Family Hall.*"

"Diego, with a commitment of $100,000, you could underwrite our animal rescue and rehabilitation center for the next five years. We'd be proud to recognize your family as the founding sponsors — helping save and care for thousands of animals who deserve a second chance."

Story of Success

I once asked a family to consider naming a children's wing of the hospital I was working at in honor of their late daughter. The moment I framed it, the room went quiet. Her mother teared up and said, "That would mean the world to us, to know her name will live on here, helping kids for years to come."

They made the gift, and at the dedication, their entire extended family showed up. It wasn't about the plaque on the wall; it was about creating a place where her memory could inspire hope and healing.

That's the **Recognition Ask**. It ties generosity to legacy in a way that feels deeply personal.

Pitfalls to Avoid

- **Overemphasizing the name.** If you make it sound like the gift is only about signage, it cheapens the moment. It's about legacy, not letters on a wall.
- **Rushing the conversation.** Recognition is intimate and

emotional. Treat it with care and give the donor space to process.

- **Failing to steward the honor.** A recognition ask isn't finished with the check. Dedications, anniversaries, and continued acknowledgment matter.

The **Recognition Ask** is effective because it enables donors to connect their personal stories to your mission. It's not just about honoring the past; it's about inspiring the future.

Chapter Twelve:
The Big Vision Ask
(For Donors Who Want to Change the World)

Some donors don't get excited by incremental change. They want to be part of something sweeping, something bold enough to transform an entire community, field, or generation. The **Big Vision Ask** gives them that chance.

This style of ask is about painting a picture of the future that is bigger than what your organization can achieve on its own. It's about inviting the donor into a world of possibility and saying, "Together, we can do this."

These are your visionary leaders. These are your philanthropists who ask, "What would it take to solve this once and for all?" Imagine the people who want their giving to ripple far beyond their own lifetime.

When to Use It

- With donors who are motivated by scale, transformation, and bold futures.
- At campaign launches, catalytic moments, or inflection points in your organization's story.
- When the project or initiative has the potential to expand your mission's reach or impact significantly.

Verbiage Examples

"Olivia, with $5M, you could launch a cancer research institute that will put our city at the forefront of discovery. Can we count on you for this?"

"Anthony, a $2M gift would allow us to build the housing, services, and support network to make youth homelessness a thing of the past in this county. Will you come alongside us?"

"Grace, your $1.5 million gift would make it possible to bring mental health services into every public school in our district."

"Dmitri, with $850,000, we can create a national model for climate-smart farming that will transform how small farms operate across the country."

Story of Success

One of my coaching clients leads a small performing arts organization. For years, they scraped by on ticket sales and small gifts, but she dreamed bigger. She wanted to restore a historic theater downtown, not just to bring performances back, but to turn it into a community hub for families, students, and local artists.

When she sat down with a longtime patron, she didn't start with construction estimates or fundraising totals. She said, "Imagine walking into this theater two years from now. Imagine families filling these seats, kids experiencing live music for the first time, and local artists finally having a stage worthy of their work. That's what this restoration will mean for our city, and with your leadership gift, you could help bring it back to life."

The donor paused, smiled, and said, "Now that's a vision I can get behind." Within weeks, she committed to donating $2.5 million, the largest gift in the organization's history.

That's the **Big Vision Ask**. It gives donors a chance to dream bigger than they ever have before.

Pitfalls to Avoid

- **Going small.** If you pitch a donor with big-vision tendencies on a minor project, they'll disengage. Match their appetite for scope.
- **Drowning in details.** Vision donors want inspiration, not a line-item budget. Save the spreadsheets for later.

- **Overpromising.** Big vision doesn't mean fantasy. Donors can tell the difference between the ambitious and the impossible.
- **Failing to connect to the donor's values.** A soaring vision only works if it resonates with what they care most about.
- **Making it your dream, not theirs.** Donors want to be co-architects of the future, not passive funders of your master plan.

The **Big Vision Ask** works because it invites donors into a story bigger than themselves — a story where their generosity writes the next chapter of history.

Chapter Thirteen:
The Challenge/Matching Ask
(For Those Who Like to Inspire Others)

Some donors don't just want to give quietly. They want their gift to *have a greater impact*. They love the idea of leverage, of using their generosity to inspire others, create urgency, and multiply impact.

The **Challenge/Matching Ask** gives them that chance. It frames their gift as the spark that ignites a fire — the lead domino that gets others moving. For donors with a natural bent toward leadership, this ask is irresistible.

This is for business leaders and entrepreneurs who understand leverage, sustainability, and scaling. Remember your community influencers who love rallying others. Picture your donors who say things like, "I'll give if it encourages others to step up, too."

When to Use It

- With donors who enjoy motivating others or being seen as leaders.
- At moments when you want to rally participation (campaigns, anniversaries, or crises).
- When urgency and momentum are key to success.

Verbiage Examples

"Cheryl, we're thinking about a creative way to spice up our year-end efforts. With a $250,000 gift, you could issue a challenge that triples every dollar given in December. Your gift would inspire hundreds of others to join you. How does that sound?"

"Malik, your $100,000 investment could be structured as a matching gift

— every family who gives sees their generosity instantly doubled because of you.”

“Howard, your $50,000 challenge could help us grow the next generation of donors. We’d like to take your $50,000 gift and find 50 new donors at $1,000 each. Is this something you could get behind?”

Story of Success

At one of my jobs, I struggled to secure donors at the $10,000 level. We had some heavy hitters who were giving millions, and then thousands of donors who contributed under $2,500. You could fit the Pacific Ocean between the two groups.

I went to a board member, one who really understood sustainability. He led a large, national company and was fiercely devoted to the success of the organization I worked for. When we met, I told him my challenge. I explained that we needed to grow the next generation of major donors.

“Bruce, would you consider making a $1 million gift? I’d like to leverage it as a match and find 100 new people to give at the $10,000 level?”

He leaned back in his office chair, chuckled, and said, “I appreciate the creativity. I’ll do it.”

After he committed, I asked him if he would match each donor’s designation as well. So, if someone gave $10,000 to one program, he’d match with $10,000 to that particular program. If someone gave $10,000 unrestricted, he’d match it to general operations. If someone earmarked for an endowment, his $10,000 match would go there, too.

“Yes,” he said. “I see the value of people wanting to give to what they care about most and feel connected. That’s how you scale initiatives. I’m happy to match wherever they donate.” Then he told me to get to work! (Fundraiser, isn’t he a gem?!)

That's the power of the **Challenge/Matching Ask**. It gives the donor the satisfaction of seeing their generosity multiplied and their leadership recognized.

Pitfalls to Avoid

- **Forgetting to follow through.** If you frame it as a challenge, you must run the campaign and show the donor the results.
- **Making it sound like a gimmick.** This isn't a BOGO sale at the mall; it's about leverage and leadership. Frame it with dignity.
- **Overcomplicating the mechanics.** If the matching rules are confusing, you'll frustrate both the donor and those you're trying to inspire.
- **Failing to report back.** Challenge donors want to know they sparked something bigger. If you don't show them the ripple effect, you'll miss the point.

The **Challenge/Matching Ask** is effective because it allows donors to see their dollars do double duty. For those who love to inspire others, it's not just a gift — it's a legacy of leadership.

Chapter Fourteen:
The Multi-Year Commitment Ask
(For Those Who Think Long-Term)

Some donors want to make sure the work continues tomorrow, next year, and beyond. The **Multi-Year Commitment Ask** invites them to step into that role, not just a one-time funder, but as a partner in long-term stability.

It also helps them stretch to their highest potential. Some donors can give their largest, single gift, but need to pay it off over several years.

This style is less about the quick win and more about the steady investment. It reassures donors that their gift will have lasting power and gives your organization the ability to plan boldly for the future.

These are your long-term investors. Consider your donors who ask about sustainability or how you'll sustain your efforts after the campaign ends.

When to Use It

- When launching a new program that needs long-term stability.
- With donors who want to see sustainability built into your work.
- During campaigns where five-year pledges or recurring leadership gifts are critical.

Verbiage Examples

"Harper, your $500,000 commitment spread over five years would ensure we have the stability to launch and sustain this program with confidence."

"Jorge, would you consider $100,000 each year for the next three years? That consistency means we can serve every family without interruption."

"Monica, your $1 million pledge over five years would give us the ability to expand services steadily and responsibly."

"Elliot, with $50,000 annually for the next five years, you'd become the anchor that keeps this program thriving long after the ribbon-cutting."

Story of Success

One of my coaching clients was raising money for a new arts program. A donor was hesitant to make a large one-time gift. Instead of pushing harder, the fundraiser reframed the ask: "What if you spread your generosity over five years? That way, you'd guarantee the program doesn't just launch, but lasts." The donor relaxed immediately. "That feels doable," he said, and committed $100,000 per year for five years, $500,000 total.

That pledge not only secured funding for the program but also gave the organization the stability and confidence to expand boldly.

That's the beauty of the **Multi-Year Commitment Ask**: it meets donors where they are financially while giving your mission the steady runway it needs to grow.

Pitfalls to Avoid

- **Making it sound like installments.** This isn't layaway. It's a visionary commitment designed to have a lasting impact. Frame it that way.
- **Minimizing the total commitment.** Even though a donor may fulfill their pledge in installments, treat it as though they've already made the full gift. Don't say, "$100,000 a year," as if it's small. Say, "Your $500,000 commitment over five years is transformational." Celebrate and steward them like the major donor they are.
- **Treating it as a default option.** Not every donor should be

offered the multi-year path. Use it strategically, when stability truly matters.

- **Neglecting stewardship mid-pledge.** If you only thank them at the start and the end, you miss the chance to nurture the relationship throughout the year.

The **Multi-Year Commitment Ask** works because it appeals to the donor's long-term mindset. It's not about making a splash today; it's about building a foundation for tomorrow.

Chapter Fifteen:
The Storytelling Ask
(For Donors Who Connect Through Emotion)

Some donors need to *feel* the impact before they can fund it. They give from their heart. For them, numbers and outcomes aren't enough. They want to hear the story of a person, a family, or a community that has undergone a significant transformation.

The **Storytelling Ask** taps into this natural human response to narrative. It connects the donor to the heart of the mission by showing them the before-and-after transformation their gift can make possible.

Think empathetic listeners. Imagine the donors who tear up at gala videos. Remember, people who lean in when you say, "Let me tell you about Maria…"

When to Use It

- When you have a powerful story that clearly connects to the ask.
- With donors who respond emotionally more than analytically.
- When you want to put a face on an abstract problem.

Verbiage Examples

"Amara, last week, a mother walked through our doors with her two children. They had been sleeping in their car for three nights. We were able to get them into an emergency shelter, but our beds are full every single night. With a gift of $100,000, you could ensure that 20 more families like hers never have to sleep in their cars again."

"Julian, let me tell you about Jacob. He's a sophomore in high school who comes to our after-school center every day because home isn't a safe place for him. Here, he gets a hot meal, homework help, and a mentor who believes in him. With $50,000, we could open a second site and give 100 more kids like Jacob the same chance."

"Lila, I want to tell you about Jordan. He's nine years old and had never been to a live performance before last spring. When the curtain rose, his eyes went wide. He was in absolute awe. For weeks afterward, his teacher said he couldn't stop talking about it. With your gift of $500,000, we could open our doors to thousands more children like Jordan, giving them that same first spark of wonder the moment they see what's possible when the lights come up."

"Evelyn, when we met Maria, she was struggling to provide for her three children after leaving an abusive relationship. Through our program, she found housing, job training, and support. Your $250,000 gift could help 50 more women like Maria rebuild their lives with dignity."

Story of Success

One of my coaching clients was raising money for a youth mentoring program. She had a donor who wasn't moved by statistics or strategic plans, but who loved to hear about the kids themselves. Instead of launching into a presentation, my client told the story of Jordan, a quiet teenager who joined the program barely speaking a word. Over the course of a year, with a mentor's guidance, he became captain of the basketball team and the first in his family to apply to college.

She ended with: "Your $100,000 gift would allow us to match 50 more teens like Jordan with mentors who will change their lives."

The donor's eyes filled with tears. She said yes on the spot.

That's the Storytelling Ask. It works because it connects the donor's generosity to the heart, not just the head.

Pitfalls to Avoid

- **Telling the wrong story.** If the story doesn't tie directly to the ask, it feels manipulative.
- **Making the story too long.** A donor wants to be moved, not trapped in a novel. Keep it tight and powerful.
- **Forgetting the ask.** Stories inspire, but without a clear invitation tied to the story, the donor leaves with feelings but no next step.
- **Using generic, broad examples.** "Families in our community need help" doesn't land. "Let me tell you about Jordan."
- **Making the donor the audience, not the actor.** Donors want to feel like they can change the ending of the story, not just hear it.

The **Storytelling Ask** works because it makes giving personal. It invites the donor to step into the narrative as the one who brings about transformation.

Chapter Sixteen:
The Exclusive Opportunity Ask
(For Donors Who Love Access)

Some donors are motivated by the chance to do something special, something not available to everyone. They want to be part of a small circle, to have insider access, and to fund something no one else can.

The **Exclusive Opportunity Ask** gives them that. It frames the gift as an invitation into a rare role, a once-in-a-lifetime moment, or a project that only they can unlock.

Who are your early adopters? Who are your connectors that love insider status? You know the type: people who light up when you whisper, "I wanted to bring this to you first."

When to Use It

- When you have a unique, one-time project or naming opportunity.
- When the donor is motivated by exclusivity, leadership, or being "first in."
- When the ask aligns with the donor's passions in a way few others could match.

Verbiage Examples

"Dominic, we have a once-in-a-generation chance to purchase the land next door and double the size of our campus. With $1 million, you could be the one to make it possible — and no one else will have this opportunity."

"Isabella, before we go public, I wanted to bring this to you first. A gift of $500,000 would fund the launch of our new arts program, and you'd be the founding investor who makes it real. Is this something you'd be interested in?"

"Caleb, there's a one-time opportunity to endow this fellowship. With $250,000, you'd create the very first named position of its kind."

"Marina, we've been offered a challenge grant that only unlocks if we secure $100,000 in private funding by June. You're the first person I thought of. Would you be willing to kick us off with a $50,000 commitment?"

Story of Success

One of my coaching clients was leading a small museum. They had the rare chance to acquire a collection of artifacts that tied directly to their community's history. The catch? They had just a few months to act, or the opportunity would vanish.

She met with a longtime donor and said, "This isn't something we can take to a hundred people. This is a once-in-a-lifetime chance, and I wanted you to be the first to know. With your gift, this collection will stay here, in this community, forever."

The donor's eyes widened. "You mean I could be the one to keep this history alive?" He wrote the check.

That's the Exclusive Opportunity Ask. It works because it makes the donor feel like they're not just giving; they're seizing a rare and irreplaceable moment.

Pitfalls to Avoid

- **Overusing the word "exclusive."** If everything is exclusive, nothing is. Save this ask for when it's truly rare.
- **Failing to deliver on the promise.** If you say they'll be first or special and then shop the same opportunity around, you'll destroy trust.
- **Sounding like a gimmick.** "Limited time only!" is for

infomercials, not philanthropy. Frame exclusivity with authenticity and respect.

- **Not tying it to their passion.** Exclusivity is meaningless if the project doesn't align with what the donor truly cares about.

The **Exclusive Opportunity Ask** is effective because it offers donors something rare: the sense that they are uniquely positioned to make this happen. It's not just generosity; it's significance.

Chapter Seventeen:
The Negotiator Ask
(For Donors Who Love the Back-and-Forth)

Some donors love the dance. They aren't content to simply say yes or no; they want to sit across from you, kick the tires, ask the tough questions, and feel like they've struck a deal. The **Negotiator's Ask** is about meeting them in that energy.

This isn't about haggling; it's about recognizing that some donors experience giving as a dialogue. They aim to counter, reframe, or shape the opportunity to make it feel like a win-win.

These are your attorneys who love negotiations or your business leaders who thrive in the boardroom. Think donors who chuckle and say, "So what's your best offer?"

When to Use It

- With donors who are naturally transactional and strategic.
- When you have the flexibility to adapt the gift structure or recognition.
- When the relationship is strong enough to withstand some spirited back-and-forth.

Verbiage Examples

"Victor, you've been with us for more than a decade. What would it take to get you to $1 million this year?"

"Leon, you've already done so much for this program. If I asked you to stretch to $250,000, how could we structure it so it feels right for you?"

"Ruth, you've told me before that you like to make your gifts work hard. If I brought you a $500,000 opportunity, what would you need to see from me to make it happen?"

Story of Success

One of my coaching clients was raising money for a new housing initiative. She met with a donor known for being tough in negotiations, someone who never agreed to the first number put on the table. This was an attorney who brought the "attorney-ness" to every conversation.

Instead of fearing the pushback, she leaned into it. She said, "The full project will cost $2.5 million. What would it take to get you to lead the campaign with a $1 million commitment?"

The donor immediately countered: "I'll do $750,000, but only if you can find someone else or a group of people to match it."

My client didn't flinch. She smiled and said, "Deal."

Within three months, a couple of donors stepped forward with the match, and suddenly, $1.5 million was secured.

That's the **Negotiator Ask.** It works because it lets the donor feel like they've had a hand in shaping the terms while still moving the mission forward.

Pitfalls to Avoid

- **Taking it personally.** Pushback isn't rejection; it's just part of the conversation for these donors.
- **Being unprepared.** If you don't know your numbers or can't pivot, you'll lose credibility fast. Negotiators respect sharpness.
- **Caving too quickly.** If you fold at the first counter, you signal weakness. Stand strong in your value.

- **Framing it adversarially.** This isn't about "beating" the donor; it's about co-creating a gift structure that works for both sides.
- **Not knowing your bottom line.** Always go in knowing what you can flex on and what you can't. Otherwise, you risk giving away more than you should.

The **Negotiator Ask** works because it makes the donor feel engaged, respected, and powerful — and when handled well, it can unlock gifts bigger than you ever expected.

Part III:

· · · · · · · · · ·

The Mastery

Chapter Eighteen:
The Objections Playbook

If there's one thing that keeps most fundraisers from asking, it's this: the fear of hearing "no."

That fear is real. When you ask for a gift, you put yourself in a vulnerable position. You're not just tossing out a number; you're inviting someone into a partnership. And in that moment, it feels like their answer is a judgment on you, your worth, or your ability as a fundraiser. It's no wonder it makes your stomach flip.

Here's the truth: objections are the crux of the fear. Fundraisers tell themselves, "What if they say no? What if I can't recover? What if I ruin the relationship? What if they get mad at me? What if they quit giving to the organization?" And so, instead of asking, they delay. They over-cultivate. They avoid the very moment that could unlock transformational generosity.

Here's the good news: objections aren't stop signs. They're conversation starters. When a donor pushes back, it doesn't mean you've failed. It means they're engaged enough to wrestle with the decision.

The late, great Jerry Panas, in his amazing book: Asking: A 59-minute Guide to Everything Board Members, Volunteers, and Staff Must Know to Secure the Gift, talks about this in great depth. The key is not to fear objections but to get curious about them.

Ask questions to understand the source of the hesitation. Is it the program? Do they not feel deeply connected to the specific initiative you've presented? Is it the institution? Do they need to see stronger leadership, or do they need to hear from your executive director or board chair? Is it the timing? Would it help if they could pledge their gift over a couple of years instead of all at once? Or is it simply the wrong moment in their life to make this decision?

When you start asking questions instead of panicking, the dynamic shifts. You're no longer trying to push past resistance; you're trying to understand it. That builds trust, diffuses fear, and often reveals a path forward.

And this is where your power as a fundraiser comes in. If you have responses ready in your back pocket, the fear melts away. You're no longer bracing for rejection; you're ready for dialogue. You don't have to panic or scramble. You can listen, respond with confidence, and keep the relationship moving forward.

That's what this playbook is for. Below you'll find the most common objections you'll hear in major gift work, and clear, practical responses that keep the door open. Think of it as your toolkit for turning "no" into "not yet," and "hesitation" into "consideration."

Money Objections

Donor Objection	How to Respond
"That's more than I can give."	"I understand. Thank you for considering it. What amount feels comfortable and meaningful to you right now?"
"I've already made a lot of commitments this year."	"Of course. How about we explore a multi-year pledge so it fits with your other commitments?"
"I can't give it all at once."	"Completely understand. Would spreading it out over three or five years make it easier?"

Timing Objections

Donor Objection	How to Respond
"This just isn't a good time."	"I hear you. When would be a better time for us to revisit this conversation?"
"The market is down right now."	"Absolutely. Many donors are structuring gifts with appreciated assets or over multiple years. Would you like to talk through some of those options?"
"Ask me again in six months."	"I'd be happy to. How about we go ahead and schedule a follow-up now so it's on both our calendars?"

Fit Objections

Donor Objection	How to Respond
"That program isn't really my passion."	"I appreciate that. Which areas of our work most align with your interests?"
"I want my gift to make a bigger impact."	"That makes sense. Let's explore the projects where your gift could be most catalytic."
"I don't want my gift to be used for overhead."	"I understand. Let me show you how overhead actually fuels impact. It's the backbone of our programming."

Trust & Organizational Objections

Donor Objection	How to Respond
"I'm not sure your leadership is strong enough."	"Thank you for your honesty. Let me share how our board and leadership team are guiding this initiative. Whose perspective would help you feel more confident: our CEO, board chair, or program lead?"
"I've heard concerns about your finances."	"Transparency is important. Would it be helpful if I walked you through our financials so you can see where every dollar goes?"
"How do I know this will last?"	"That's a fair question. Here's our sustainability plan and how we'll steward your gift long term."

Personal Objections

Donor Objection	How to Respond
"I need to talk to my spouse/family first."	"Of course. Would it be helpful if we had a conversation together?"
"I'm just not sure right now."	"I respect that. How about I circle back in a few weeks to give you time to think?"
"I'm worried this will set a precedent."	"That's understandable. We'd be clear about what this gift covers, and future asks would always be in alignment with your goals."

The Golden Rule of Objections

Every objection is really a clue. Instead of fearing it, get curious. Ask yourself: *Is this about the program? The institution? The timing? Or the way I presented the ask?* When you respond with curiosity instead of defensiveness, you turn an objection into the next step of the relationship.

"Off-the-Wall (and Occasionally Scandalous) Objections"

Not every objection is polite or predictable. Every once in a great while, donors throw out something so blunt, scandalous, or out of left field that you can feel the air leave the room. Here are a few real-life curveballs I've heard (or that my coaching clients have told me about), and how you can still keep your composure.

Curveball Objection	How to Respond
"I don't like your CEO's vision."	"Thank you for being candid. Can you tell me more about what's not resonating? Additionally, whose perspective would you trust to hear more from: our board chair or a program leader?"
"I'll give if you fire so-and-so."	"I appreciate your honesty. Personnel decisions are handled carefully by leadership. Is there another area of work where you'd feel comfortable directing your support?"
"Call me when the stock market hits 30,000."	(Smile) "I hear you. Markets do play a big role. In the meantime, would you like to explore pledge options that give you flexibility? A multi-year commitment makes it feel less dependent on market swings."
"What's in this for me? Box seats, perks, or introductions?"	"While recognition is part of giving, what excites most of our donors is the lasting impact they create. Beyond benefits, what would feel meaningful to you?"
"Why should I give when your staff salaries are so high?"	"That's a fair question. Our team is our greatest asset, and I'd love to show you how their work drives impact. Would it be helpful if I walked you through how our budget supports outcomes?"
"I don't give to organizations with female leadership."	(Deep breath) "I appreciate your honesty, though I don't share that view. If that's a dealbreaker for you, I understand. But our leadership is a source of strength we're proud of."

Chapter Nineteen:
From Script to Second Nature

By now, you've got a toolkit of asks at your fingertips. But let's be honest: reading them on a page is one thing; saying them out loud to a donor in real time is something else entirely.

Fundraiser, this is where most people get stuck. They know the words, but when the moment comes, nerves take over. Suddenly, the clear ask they practiced turns into a rambling half-sentence or disappears altogether.

The goal of this chapter is simple: to help you move from script to second nature. You don't need to memorize every word; you need to practice until the rhythm, tone, and confidence of your ask feel like they're yours.

Why Practice Matters

Think about athletes or musicians. They don't wait until game day or concert night to try things out for the first time. They practice until the moves are muscle memory. Fundraising is no different. The more you rehearse, the more natural the words will feel when you're across the table from a donor.

How to Practice Without Feeling Awkward

- **Say it out loud.** Reading silently in your head is not the same as speaking. Words sound different when you give them voice.
- **Record yourself.** Your phone is your best coach. Play it back, listen for hesitation or filler words, then refine. Delete when you're done if that makes you feel better.
- **Practice with safe people.** Partner, best friend, mom, someone who will cheer you on, not harshly critique you.
- **Use the mirror test.** Watch your body language. Are you

shrinking back? Smiling? Making eye contact? Your presence matters as much as your words.

- **Role-play with colleagues.** Trade roles so you can both sharpen your delivery and practice responding to donor reactions.
- **Practice silence.** Deliver the ask, then force yourself to sit in ten seconds of quiet. Get comfortable with the pause; it's the part that feels longest and matters most.

Building Confidence Over Time

At first, practice might feel clunky. You'll stumble, over-explain, or sound scripted. That's normal. Keep going. With repetition, you'll find your natural voice inside the script.

I used to play the same pump-up song in my car before every solicitation. It was my ritual, my way of telling myself, you've got this. Over time, the combination of practice and routine made me calm and confident in the room.

The more you practice, the less you'll feel like you're "performing" a script. Instead, you'll feel like you're having a clear, courageous conversation, which is exactly what an ask should be.

Pitfalls to Avoid

- **Sounding memorized.** Scripts are training wheels, not the endgame. Don't sound robotic.
- **Avoiding practice because it feels silly.** Better to feel silly in front of your mirror than panicked in front of a donor.
- **Practicing only once.** Repetition is what builds confidence. Do it until the words feel like yours.
- **Practicing only the easy parts.** Don't skip the silence or the specific number; those are the moments that matter most.

The goal isn't perfection; the goal is confidence. When you've practiced enough that the words feel natural, you'll walk into the room not just ready to ask, but ready to enjoy the moment.

Helpful Hints from the Ask Trenches

- **Never solicit one spouse without the other.** If the gift requires a joint decision, you want both of them in the room. Otherwise, it delays the decision.

- **Avoid asking in a public space.** Coffee shops are great for lattes, not six-figure asks. You don't want the barista in your business. Try meeting at the donor's home or at your organization.

- **Bring the right team.** If your CEO or board chair has the magic sauce with this donor, bring them. You don't always have to be both the case-maker and the closer.

- **Have a backup program or initiative in your pocket.** If they don't bite on the project you lead with, pivot gracefully to another area of your mission.

- **Follow their cues.** If they're leaning in, don't over-explain. If they're hesitating, ask a clarifying question instead of plowing ahead.

- **Debrief right away.** After the meeting, jot down everything while it's fresh: tone, responses, exact wording. That becomes gold for your next step.

Chapter Twenty:
Asking as a Joyful Act

At the end of the day, Fundraiser, here's what I want you to carry with you: asking is not something to dread; it's something to celebrate.

Yes, it can feel scary. Yes, it can feel vulnerable. But asking for a major gift isn't about twisting someone's arm or "getting" money out of them. It's about opening a door to joy, for the donor, your mission, and for you.

Think about it. Donors are looking for meaning. They want to use their resources to change lives, strengthen communities, and leave a legacy. You get to be the one who helps them do that. You are the bridge between their generosity and the impact they long to make.

Reframing the Fear

When fear creeps in, when your stomach flips or your palms sweat, remember this: the ask is not about you. It's about them. It's about giving the donor the chance to live out their values in a tangible way. Without the ask, they never get that opportunity.

The Energy of a Yes

There is nothing like it. A donor says yes, and suddenly new programs launch, families are fed, patients are cared for, students are educated, and communities are transformed. The energy of that moment is electric, and you get to be there, front row, when it happens.

Even the No's

Even when a donor says no, it's not failure; it's clarity. It's one step closer to understanding what matters to them, what timing is right, or what project will light them up. Every no is part of a longer conversation that keeps the relationship alive.

Fundraiser, You Get to Do This

You get to invite people into something bigger than themselves. You get to sit at tables where lives are changed. You get to witness generosity in its purest form.

Asking is not a chore. It's not a burden. It's not a necessary evil. Asking is a joyful act. It's a privilege, a calling, and when you see it this way, one of the best parts of the job.

So, walk into that next donor meeting with courage, with confidence, and with joy. Because you don't have to ask for the gift; you get to.

You deserve a parade for your hard work. Don't ever forget that.

Closing Note from Mary

Fundraiser, if you've made it this far, you've done something bold: you've leaned into the part of fundraising that most people avoid. You've opened yourself up to the vulnerability of the ask, and you've chosen to get better at it.

I want you to hear this from me: you are capable of this work. You don't have to be perfect, you don't have to get every ask right, and you don't have to carry the weight of every "no." What matters is that you show up with courage, clarity, and heart.

For years, I knew only one way to ask, and I used it with every donor, regardless of their style or personality. It wasn't until I learned to tailor the ask to meet donors where they are that everything shifted. Suddenly, the conversations felt lighter. The yeses came easier. The relationships went deeper.

That's what I want for you: to experience the joy of sitting across from a donor, saying the words with confidence, and watching their eyes light up as they step into something bigger than themselves.

This book isn't just a toolkit of scripts; it's a reminder that you are not alone in the asking. Every fundraiser before you felt the nerves, the fear, and the thrill of the yes. And every fundraiser after you will, too.

So go make the ask. Say the donor's name. Name the number. Paint the vision. Then sit back and let them step into generosity.

Because at the end of the day, this isn't about money; it's about joy. And you, Fundraiser, get to be the one who carries that joy into the world.

With gratitude and cheering you on,
Mary

P.S. Don't postpone joy! Go call a donor right now…

About the Author

Mary Petersen thinks about fundraising all day. She's spent over 25 years in the major gift trenches, coaching fundraisers, making the asks, and celebrating the joyful yeses that transform communities.

When she's not helping nonprofits raise millions, Mary can be found dancing at her desk between Zoom calls or curating her playlist (which could easily be mistaken for that of a teenage girl).

She's a fierce Taylor Swift fan, incense burner, candy enthusiast, and a gym member who proudly goes… well, let's just say *sometimes*. Her husband affectionately calls her "crunchy," and her two golden retrievers, Todd and Kevin, run the household (and frequently make cameos in her video courses).

She devours books (especially Ken Follett, who has been known to derail her workweek), and is married to the most perfect man in the world (who lovingly accepts her quirks).

At the end of the day, Mary believes fundraising is not about money; it's about joy. And she's here to help you experience that joy, one confident ask at a time.

A Special Thank You!

Every book is a community effort, and *What to Say* is no exception.

To my dear colleagues for saying yes to this journey with me: you carved out time in your busy lives, read early drafts with care, and gave me the kind of honest feedback that made this book sharper, stronger, and more useful for fundraisers everywhere. This book is better because of you.

My sincerest appreciation goes to:

Evan Abood
Duke Bonaventura
Robert J. Brodrick, PhD
Nick Dalsey, MBA, AVP Philanthropy
Erin Frerichs, RCE Director of Development
Kelly Grattan, PhD, MBA, AP(R), CFRE
Linda Vinz Hummel
Daniel Johnson, Chief Consultant, Next Level Nonprofits
Gunnar Johnson
Patricia Johnston
Tom Keith, MBA, MED
Clarke W. Leslie
Isabel Lowney Brouhard, CFRE
Kristin Mabrouk
William Myatt, PhD, Founding Owner of Major Gift Solutions
Terry Okken, Director of Advancement
Anthony G. Padgett, CFRE
Tim Petersen
Brian Rosenbaum
Desiree Saunders, Chief Development Officer – Handy Inc.
Carol TeBockhorst, Director of Philanthropic Giving, Make-A-Wish Iowa
Heidi Totten, Founder, 100 Humanitarians International
Fran Tucker
Shay Upadhyay, CFRE
Lindsey Vanzant
Aude Wilkins
Heather Withrow, Executive Director